Titanic!

PAUL SHIPTON

Level 3

Series Editors: Andy Hopkins and Jocelyn Potter

Pearson Education Limited
Edinburgh Gate, Harlow,
Essex CM20 2JE, England
and Associated Companies throughout the world.

ISBN 0 582 438373

First published 2001

Design by Neil Alexander
Printed and bound in Denmark by Norhaven A/S, Viborg

Published by Pearson Education Limited in association with
Penguin Books Ltd, both companies being subsidiaries of Pearson Plc

Photograph acknowledgements:
Kobal: pp. 3, 37, 38 and 39; Corbis: pp. 9, 31 and 32: Ronald Grant: pp. 15, 36, 37 and 39;
Rex: p. 35.

For a complete list of the titles available in the Penguin Readers series please write to your
local Pearson Education office or to: Marketing Department, Penguin Longman Publishing,
5 Bentinck Street, London W1M 5RN.

contents

INTRODUCTION

Parents said goodbye to their children. Husbands kissed their wives for the last time. One woman's husband told her, "You go. I will stay." The lifeboat left, and she never saw him again.

There were many examples of bravery on the *Titanic* on the night of April 14, 1912. Some of the crew and passengers worked all night to save other people. They chose to stay on the ship until the end. Other passengers thought only about saving themselves. They fought to get into the lifeboats.

Some people think that the *Titanic* showed people at their best and at their worst. Maybe this is why the disaster is still famous. The ship sank in the North Atlantic over seventy-five years ago. But almost everybody in the world today knows the name of the *Titanic.*

So what really happened that night? Why did the ship hit an iceberg? Why didn't another ship save the passengers? How many people survived, and how many died?

You will find the answers in this book. But remember that the disaster is more than just a story in a history book. It happened a long time ago, but some old people today can still remember it. There were many kinds of people on the ship—rich and poor, young and old. Each person had hopes and dreams. When the ship sank, hundreds died. Their hopes and dreams died with them.

Paul Shipton lives and works in the United States and writes mostly for younger people. *Ghost in the Guitar* is another of his Penguin Readers.

The Ship of Dreams

How much do you already know?

Try to answer these questions about the *Titanic*. You can find all of the answers in this book.

1 In 1912, the *Titanic* was the biggest ship that was ever built. How long was it?
   a 269 meters (882 feet)   b 149 meters (489 feet)
   c 328 meters (1,076 feet)
2 What was the name of the ship's captain?
   a Ismay   b Smith   c Lightoller
3 How many people died on the *Titanic*?
   a 500   b more than 1,500   c 250
4 Where was the *Titanic* traveling to?
   a Southampton   b Nova Scotia   c New York
5 There were over 2,200 people on the ship. How many people could the lifeboats carry?
   a 2,278   b 1,178   c 1,923
6 How many third-class passengers died?
   a 10%   b 25%   c 75%
7 Which ship picked up the survivors?
   a *Carpathia*   b *Olympic*   c *Californian*
8 After the accident, when was the *Titanic* seen again?
   a 1985   b 1959   c 1995
9 James Cameron made the 1997 movie *Titanic*. Which of these movies did he also make?
   a *Saving Private Ryan*   b *The Terminator*   c *Gladiator*
10 How many Oscars did the movie *Titanic* win?
   a 5   b 8   c 11

(The answers are on page 44.)

The king of the world!

James Cameron was the big winner at Oscar night in Los Angeles in March 1998. His 1997 movie was named Best Picture, winning ten other Oscars, too. As Cameron held up the Oscar, he repeated a famous line from the movie: "I'm the king of the world!" He later joked that "size does matter."

It was a dream that Cameron had for a long time. He loved history and he was always interested in the story of the *Titanic*. Cameron's early movies—for example, *The Terminator* and *Aliens*—were full of action. *Titanic* had plenty of action, too, but the heart of the movie was a love story. Cameron chose two young actors for this.

Leonardo DiCaprio played Jack Dawson. Born in 1974, DiCaprio was first seen on TV at the age of five. He became famous in the 1990s with movies like *What's Eating Gilbert Grape?* and *This Boy's Life*. Work on Cameron's *Titanic* was long and difficult for DiCaprio.

Kate Winslet played Jack's lover, Rose. The British actress was also born in 1974. Winslet was not interested in small parts in Hollywood movies. She wanted to act in the theater. But soon Kate was in the biggest movie that was ever made.

While Cameron was making the movie, not everybody was so sure about its success. It took a long time to make the movie. As it continued, the cost went up and up. It finally cost between $185,000,000 and $200,000,000. The movie's opening was changed from summer of 1997 to December. Many newspapers and magazines wrote stories about the movie like "*Titanic* Sinks."

Titanic was more expensive than any other movie:

* For the first part, Cameron filmed the real *Titanic* at the bottom of the ocean. He had to go down to the ship in a submarine twelve times.
* Cameron filmed most of the movie on a model that was almost as big as the *Titanic*. He wanted everything on the ship to be like the real *Titanic*. Clothes, furniture, machines—everything had to be exactly right.

Not all newspapers and magazines liked the movie. One called it "dead in the water." But people around the world loved it. The world's most expensive movie became the biggest success. It earned over $1,600,000,000!

Work on Cameron's Titanic *was long and difficult.*

The Biggest Ship in

The biggest and the best!

In the 1900s, more and more people wanted to travel across the Atlantic Ocean. The ships became bigger and better, as ship companies fought hard for customers. In 1907, the White Star Line decided to build the biggest and the best of all. The company planned to make three ships. Their names said a lot about them—*Olympic*, *Titanic*, and *Gigantic*.

Next to the *Titanic*, most other ships seemed small. It was 269 meters (882 feet) long. At the time, the tallest building in the world was only 229 meters (750 feet).

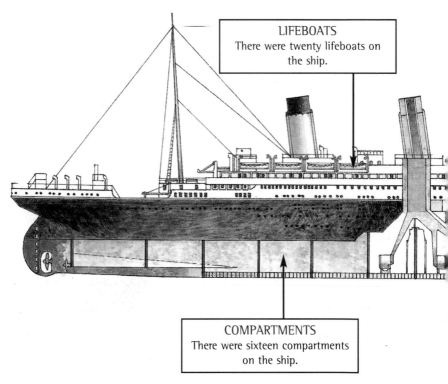

LIFEBOATS
There were twenty lifeboats on the ship.

COMPARTMENTS
There were sixteen compartments on the ship.

the World

Everyone thought that the ship was also very safe. There were sixteen compartments. In an accident, big metal doors could close and then no water could get from one compartment to another. The ship was even able to float with the first 4 compartments full of water!

The *Titanic* became the famous "unsinkable ship." Nobody seemed to worry about another important fact. The ship could carry more than 3,000 passengers, but it only had lifeboats for 1,178 people.

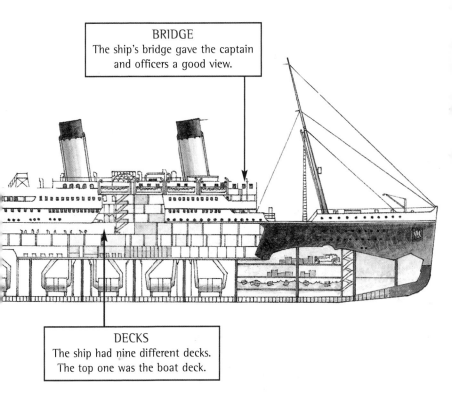

BRIDGE
The ship's bridge gave the captain and officers a good view.

DECKS
The ship had nine different decks. The top one was the boat deck.

"That ship is going to sink!"

Can some people see the future? Can dreams ever show what is going to happen? A few strange things happened before the *Titanic* sailed for the first time in 1912.

Strange Books

* In 1898, Morgan Robertson wrote a book called *Futility, or The Wreck on the Titan*. The book told the story of a ship crossing the Atlantic. It hit an iceberg and sank. Almost all of the passengers died because there weren't enough lifeboats.
* Six years earlier, in 1892, William T. Stead wrote *From the Old World to the New*. In that story, too, a ship hit an iceberg and sank. Another ship picked up the survivors. The captain's name was E. J. Smith—the name of the *Titanic*'s captain. Twenty years later, Stead traveled on the real *Titanic*. He didn't survive.

Dreams and Bad Feelings

* The Adelmans were planning to return to America on the *Titanic*. Suddenly, Mrs. Adelman had a terrible feeling of danger. She and her husband didn't travel on the *Titanic*.
* Mrs. Blanche Marshall watched the *Titanic* from an island near Southampton. "That ship is going to sink before it reaches America," she said. "I can see hundreds of people in the icy water."

The *Titanic* left Southampton, on the south coast of England, at noon on April 10, 1912. Even at the start of the trip, the *Titanic* had bad luck. There was almost an accident in the first minutes of the trip.

The danger passed, but for some people this was a bad start to the famous ship's first trip across the Atlantic. Some people said, "It's bad luck!"

A The *Titanic* sailed past two other ships, the *Oceanic* and the *New York*.

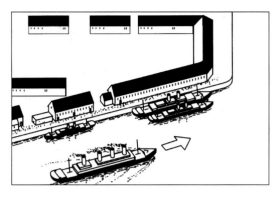

B Because the *Titanic* was so big, the *New York* was pulled closer toward it. The ropes broke on the smaller ship. It began to float toward the *Titanic*.

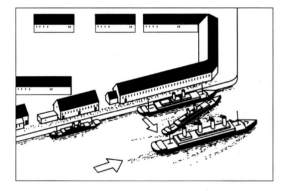

C Luckily, a small boat was able to tie a rope onto the *New York*. It pulled the smaller ship out of the way.

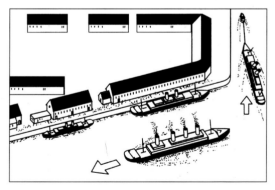

At this time of year, there was also a danger of icebergs in the North Atlantic. But the *Titanic*'s captain, Edward Smith, wasn't really worried about ice—this was the unsinkable *Titanic*!

The Queen of the Ocean

The *Titanic* was able to carry more than 3,000 people, but there were only 2,207 people on the ship for its first trip.

First class: 322 passengers
Second class: 275 passengers
Third class: 712 passengers
Crew: 898 people

The different classes didn't mix on the ship. They slept, lived, and ate on different decks. Of course, the first-class passengers were on the higher decks. The second-class passengers were in the middle. Then came the third-class passengers, at the bottom.

First Class
The White Star Line called the *Titanic* "the Queen of the Ocean." For first-class passengers, life on the *Titanic* was as comfortable as life in the most expensive hotels in Europe and America. There were hundreds of servants to look after them. Their private rooms were large and comfortable. They could enjoy a swimming pool, a library, Turkish baths, and excellent restaurants and bars.

Some of the richest people in the world were on the ship. In fact, American John Jacob Astor IV was possibly the richest of all. In 1912 he had $87 million. (That is more than $1,500,000,000 today.)

Bruce Ismay, the president of the White Star Line and Thomas Andrews, the ship's builder, were also on the *Titanic*.

Second Class
Life for the passengers in second class was comfortable, too. In fact, second class on the *Titanic* was as nice as first-class travel on many other ships. These passengers also had a library and a few bars. They, too, could walk around on an open deck and enjoy views of the ocean.

Life was as comfortable as the life in the most expensive hotels.

Third Class

More than half of the passengers were in third class. Of course, life on these decks wasn't as comfortable. But the rooms were clean and bright.

More than 100 of the third-class passengers were from Ireland. The others came from many different countries in Europe. Most of them had the same dream. They were leaving their problems in their own countries. For them, the United States of America was the promise of a new life.

A Passenger's Story

PART 1

SEVENTEEN-YEAR-OLD JACK THAYER WAS ON THE *TITANIC* AFTER A VACATION IN EUROPE WITH HIS PARENTS.

I don't think I'll be bored on this ship!

HE USED THE SHIP'S SWIMMING POOL EVERY DAY.

A ship with a swimming pool!

ON SUNDAY EVENING, WHILE HIS PARENTS ATE DINNER WITH THE CAPTAIN, JACK ATE ALONE.

Excuse me. Can I have a light?

Of course.

THE TWO YOUNG MEN TALKED FOR A LONG TIME.

This ship's wonderful, isn't it?

I was on a ship that sank once. It was near Alaska.

THE MAN'S NAME WAS MILTON LONG. HE WAS TRAVELING HOME TO AMERICA, TOO.

The "Unsinkable

On Sunday, April 14, while the passengers enjoyed life on the *Titanic*, radio operators Jack Phillips and Harold Bride were busy. Many passengers wanted to send personal messages to friends and relatives on land. But Phillips and Bride were receiving messages from other ships also.

 Early in the afternoon, Phillips received an ice warning from a ship called the *Baltic*. It was the third warning of the day. The message was taken to the bridge, but Captain Smith didn't show it to his officers until 7:15 P.M.

 It was a cold, clear evening now. Seeing the message about ice, Second Officer Lightoller told the lookouts to watch carefully for icebergs.

 In the radio room, Jack Phillips took another message about icebergs ahead. It never reached the bridge. Phillips put it down on his desk and continued with his work.

 Phillips received another message. This one was from a ship called the *Californian*. The ship couldn't move through the ice. "Shut up, shut up," Philips said. "I'm busy."

 Lookouts Frederick Fleet and Reginald Lee were cold and tired. Suddenly, Fleet saw a large, black shape in the ocean. He rang the warning three times and telephoned the bridge.

"Iceberg right ahead," he told Sixth Officer James Moody.

Ship" Sinks

On the bridge, First Officer William Murdoch had to act fast. He turned the ship left, hoping to miss the iceberg. he also ordered the crew to stop the ship.

The iceberg was thirty meters higher than the top decks. Some ice fell onto the deck as the ship passed it. But nothing broke. It was a different story under the water. The iceberg hit the side of the ship, making a few long holes below the water. Many passengers heard the noise, but it wasn't very loud. Nobody knew it yet, but this was the beginning of the end for the *Titanic*.

Captain Smith hurried to the bridge.

"What have we hit?" he asked Murdoch.

"An iceberg, sir," replied the First Officer.

Soon Bruce Ismay of the White Star Line was on the bridge, too. Fourth Officer Joseph Boxhall went to check the lower decks. Fifteen minutes later, he reported, "Water is coming in."

Captain Smith and the ship's builder, Thomas Andrews, went below to check. Andrews immediately understood the terrible danger. The ship could float with water in the four compartments at the front, but there was water in five of the compartments. There was no hope. The *Titanic* was sinking.

There was only one thing that Captain Smith could do now. Just after midnight, he ordered the crew to prepare the lifeboats.

"Women and children first!"

After Smith gave the order, the crew started to wake the passengers. They told them to put on their lifebelts and warm clothes. Passengers should go to the boat deck.

At first, many of them didn't believe the danger—of course, the *Titanic* couldn't sink! Some of the first lifeboats were almost empty. There were twelve people in one boat for seventy people.

As the front end of the *Titanic* sank lower and lower in the water, more passengers began to understand the danger. But they still didn't know the most terrible fact of all. There were more than 2,200 people on the *Titanic*, but the ship had lifeboats for only 1,178!

Parents said goodbye to their children. Husbands kissed their wives for the last time. One woman's husband told her, "You go. I will stay." The lifeboat left, and she never saw him again.

- First-class passenger Molly Brown was put into the third lifeboat and she helped to get the boat away from the ship. Later, she saved a dying man, keeping him warm with her coat.
- An old woman, Mrs. Ida Straus, decided not to go into a lifeboat. She couldn't leave her husband. "We have lived together and we will die together," she said.
- One man put on women's clothes and tried to get into a lifeboat. The officer sent him away angrily.
- Third-class passenger Minnie Coutts didn't have enough lifebelts for her two sons. One of the crew gave his lifebelt to her. "There!" he said. "If the boat goes down, you'll remember me!"

Now there was no problem filling up the boats.

By one o'clock, the danger was clear to everybody. Now there was no problem filling up the boats and the officers had a different problem. They had to keep people away. Guns were given to the officers on the boat deck.

"Come Quick!"

While the crew began to fill the lifeboats, radio operators Jack Phillips and Harold Bride began to send messages for help. Their message was CQD—"Come quick, danger."

At first Phillips and Bride weren't worried. They even made jokes as they worked.

"You'll see your first iceberg," said Phillips with a laugh.

"The Americans will enjoy it," answered Bride. "They all like to have ice in their drinks."

The first replies came from ships that were too far away. Then Phillips heard from the *Carpathia*. The ship was traveling from New York to the Mediterranean. The *Carpathia*'s radio operator, Cyril Evans, couldn't hide his surprise. He immediately told Arthur Rostron, the captain of the *Carpathia*. Then he called the *Titanic* again. The *Carpathia* was turning around. It was coming to help. But there was a problem. The *Carpathia* was about ninety-three kilometers (58 miles) away. It could reach the *Titanic* in four hours. That was too long—the *Titanic* had less than two hours.

Now Phillips and Bride understood the danger. They continued to send messages, hoping to find a closer ship. The *Titanic* was becoming noisier and their job became harder and harder.

As they worked, Phillips and Bride started sending the new help message, SOS. The *Titanic* was the first ship that sent an SOS message. It was quicker and easier to send.

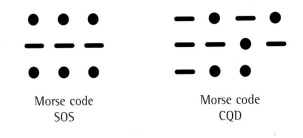

Morse code
SOS

Morse code
CQD

The two men bravely stayed in the room until it was almost the end. Their last message was sent at 2:17 A.M.. Outside on the deck, hope was growing. Captain Smith and Fourth Officer Boxhall could see the lights of a ship that was only 9.5—16 kilometers (6—10 miles) away. The crew tried to send a message to the ship with a light. Then, at 12:45 A.M., they began to send rockets high into the dark sky. They sent a rocket every five minutes. At first, the ship seemed to be coming closer. But then its lights disappeared. Hopes of help for the *Titanic* disappeared with them.

What was the ship that was so close? Why didn't it help?

◆ Some people think that it was the *Californian*. In fact, the crew of the *Californian* did see lights in the sky and the lights of a ship. But the ship seemed quite small to them. When they tried to send a message to it, there was no answer.

◆ Did the officers on the *Titanic* see a different ship? More and more people today think that it was a Norwegian fishing boat. Why didn't it help? Maybe it was breaking the law by being in the area.

"Well boys, do your best!"

After one o'clock on the morning of April 15, the *Titanic*'s front end was sinking fast. The band still played and the lights were on. But everyone knew what was happening. And there were few lifeboats left.

- A fourteen- or fifteen-year-old boy tried to hide on a lifeboat. The ship's officer pointed a gun at him. "Be a man," he said. The boy left the lifeboat.
- When one lifeboat hit the water, its ropes were still joined to the ship. Before it could get away, another lifeboat began to come down on top of it. Luckily, a crewman cut the ropes with a knife in time.

Was it true?

Many people believe that the third-class passengers were kept away from the boat decks. It is true that many of these passengers lost their lives.

Some of the crew did try to help the third-class passengers to the boats. The job wasn't easy. Passengers had to go up the ship's many decks. Many of them didn't speak English. They didn't understand the danger. Some refused to follow the crew and stayed on their deck.

Some doors were locked by the crew. Nobody really knows why. Were they following orders? Were they just afraid? But women and children from third class *were* sent to the boat deck. The most crowded lifeboat left at 1:25 A.M. with seventy people in it. Most of them were women and children from third class. But the men were still kept away from the boat deck. When they reached it at last, it was too late. Almost all the lifeboats were gone.

By two o'clock, the water was just below the boat deck. When the crew were preparing the next lifeboat, a crowd tried to climb into it. Second Officer Lightoller stopped them by waving his gun. The crew made a wall with their bodies while women and children got into the boat.

Now only two small lifeboats were left. Each boat could hold forty-seven people. They were still tied to a roof on the deck.

While the crew tried to free these last boats Captain Smith shouted to them, "Well, boys, do your best for the women and children!" Then he told them to save themselves.

There were still more than 1,500 people on the ship. Many of them looked for ways to survive. Others prepared to die.

- First-class passenger Benjamin Guggenheim came on deck in his dinner suit. "We've dressed up in our best and are prepared to go down like gentlemen," he said.

- At around 2:10 A.M., Wallace Hartley told the musicians in his band to save themselves. All eight musicians chose to stay with Hartley, and they played a final song together.

  Suddenly, the front of the ship moved more quickly down into the water. A big wave began to move up the boat deck. The end was here.

A Passenger's Story

CONTINUES . . .

"It seemed a dream."

The deck was getting steeper and steeper. It was impossible to stand. There was a terrible crashing noise as furniture and plates fell. Many people were thrown into the water. Others jumped, hoping to swim to a lifeboat.

Radio operator Harold Bride was one of the men who were trying to free the last lifeboats. As the great wave came up the deck, one boat floated away on the water upside-down. More than twenty men climbed on top of it, but Bride was under the boat and he couldn't escape. For forty-five minutes, he held onto the boat in the freezing water.

In the great ship's final minutes, the lights went out. There was no moon that night, but some light came from the stars in the clear, dark sky. Suddenly, there was a new noise. This was the loudest of all and it could only mean one thing. The ship was breaking in two. People were still falling. Others chose to jump now. One passenger spoke of the last seconds as the ship sank:

"Slowly . . . the water seemed to come up toward us . . . It seemed a dream."

At 2:20 on the morning of April 15, the "Queen of the Ocean" was gone.

At first, the people in the lifeboats were most afraid for their own lives. One crewman shouted, "Pull for your lives." But they had to decide what to do. The *Titanic* was gone and hundreds of people were in the icy water of the North Atlantic. Some were holding onto furniture. Others were trying to swim. Many were screaming for help. To the people in the lifeboats, the noise seemed to fill the night.

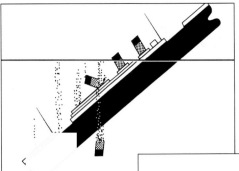

A As the front part of the ship sank, the back came up out of the water. It climbed higher and higher.

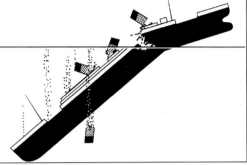

B The ship broke in two. The front part sank.

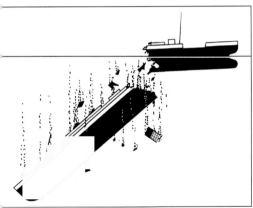

C The back part of the *Titanic* fell back. It sat flat in the water for a short time. Hope grew in some passengers. They probably thought, "It's going to float!"

D Then this part of the ship began to sink, too. Soon the back of the ship was high in the air. It didn't move for a few minutes. Then it began to sink, moving faster and faster into the dark water.

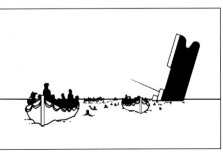

23

In the Water

The people in the lifeboats listened to all those cries for help. Imagine the terrible discussions.

You sit in the lifeboat. The cold is terrible. But you know that it is much, much worse for the people in the black water. You can hear their screams in the dark.

"They can't stay alive in the freezing water," says a man in the boat. "It's too cold."

"Our friends and relatives are dying!" shouts a woman holding a small child. "My husband stayed on the ship. We have to go back and help."

The crewman shakes his head. "We can't. If we go back, too many people will try to get into the boat. Then, we'll all die."

"We have to save ourselves now!" agrees a man at the back of the boat. He is crying as he speaks.

You listen in silence. The screams are becoming quieter, as the people in the water become weaker and weaker. Soon it will be too late.

What do you think? What was the right thing to do?

In fact, only one of the lifeboats did go back. Fifth Officer Harold Lowe ordered a search for survivors, but it was too late. When they arrived most people were dead. Only twelve people were pulled from the water.

One of the people in the water that night was young Jack Thayer.

A Passenger's Story

PART 3

JACK WAS A STRONG SWIMMER, BUT THE WATER WAS ICY.

I can't believe it. The ship is breaking in two!

Milton! Where are you?

BUT JACK NEVER SAW MILTON LONG AGAIN.

MOST OF THE MEN ON THE BOAT WERE FROM THE SHIP'S CREW.

Here, boy.

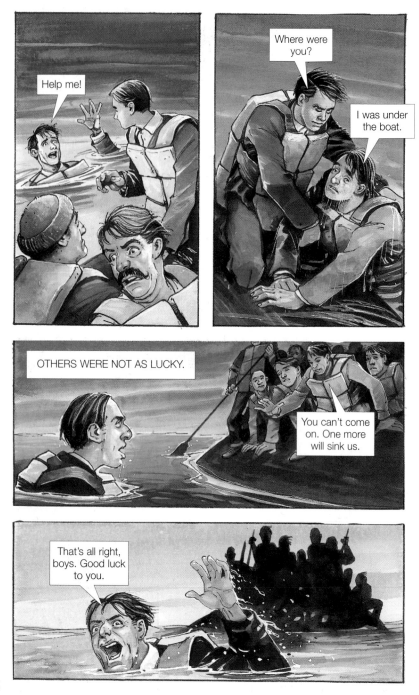

26

The *Carpathia* arrives

When he received the *Titanic*'s SOS message in the night, Captain Rostron of the *Carpathia* ordered his ship to go as fast as possible. There was a lot of ice in the area. But Rostron was a good captain. The *Carpathia* saw a rocket from one of the lifeboats at 4 A.M.—less than two hours after the *Titanic* sank.

It wasn't easy to find all of the survivors. The lifeboats covered a 6.5 kilometer (4-mile) area. It took Rostron and his crew four hours to pick up everybody. People in the boats waved and shouted. Some burned letters and papers so the *Carpathia* could see them.

Captain Rostron ordered his crew to count the survivors. They counted 705. Later, people guessed 711 or even 757 survivors. That meant that more than 1,500 of the *Titanic*'s passengers and crew died.

FIRST CLASS
Men: 54 lived; 119 died.
Women and children: 145 lived;
10 women and 1 child died.

SECOND CLASS
Men: 15 lived; 142 died.
Women and children: 104 lived;
24 died.

60% SURVIVED

42% SURVIVED

Who lived and who died?

- **Bruce Ismay**, the president of the White Star Line, escaped in one of the last lifeboats.
- **Thomas Andrews**, the ship's builder, died with the ship. He never even put his lifebelt on.
- **Captain Smith** didn't survive. There was a newspaper story about him saving a baby in the water. It probably wasn't true.
- **Harold Bride** lived. He even worked in the radio room as the *Carpathia* sailed to New York.
- **Jack Phillips** wasn't as lucky as Bride. He swam to a lifeboat but died of cold in the night.
- Second Officer **Charles Lightoller** survived. He was the last survivor who climbed onto the *Carpathia*.
- **Wallace Hartley** and the musicians in his band went down with the ship.
- **Molly Brown** lived and became famous for her bravery on the night of the disaster. In 1960 there was even a musical play about her, *The Unsinkable Molly Brown*.
- **Jack Thayer** found his mother on the *Carpathia*. His father died on the *Titanic*. He later wrote a letter to Milton Long's parents, describing their son's last hours alive.

THIRD CLASS
Men: 69 lived; 417 died.
Women and children:
105 lived; 119 died.

25% SURVIVED

24% SURVIVED

THE CREW
Men: 194 lived; 682 died.
Women: 20 lived; 3 died.

The World Cries

At first, as the *Carpathia* traveled back to New York, no messages were sent to the waiting world. Some newspapers, still believing in the "unsinkable" ship, got the story completely wrong. In their news stories, the *Titanic* was safe and all the passengers were alive.

When the news was finally known, sadness and surprise were felt around the world. Ten thousand people were waiting when the *Carpathia* arrived in New York on the evening of Thursday, April 18. Through newspapers and radio, the eyes of the world were on the ship and its survivors.

Even after the terrible accident, things were very different for first-class and third-class passengers. The survivors from first-class were taken to the best hotels in New York. But the passengers from third-class were in a new country without any money or clothes, or any of their things.

Back in the North Atlantic, a ship was picking up dead bodies from the ocean. In the next six weeks, 328 bodies were found. The crew of the *Mackay-Bennet* didn't know who most of them were. But they did know John Jacob Astor IV, possibly the richest man in the world. He was carrying a big gold ring, a gold watch, and a lot of money when he died. None of it helped him.

In Britain and the US, people were angry about the disaster. Many questions were asked.
- Why didn't Captain Smith act on warnings about ice?
- Why did Bruce Ismay survive when his passengers died?
- Why didn't the *Californian* help when they saw rockets?
- Did a Norwegian fishing ship turn away from the *Titanic*?
- Why weren't there lifeboats for all the passengers?

The eyes of the world were on the ship and its survivors.

The Mystery Children

One of the strangest stories was the *Titanic*'s mystery children. When the ship was going down, a man passed his two young sons into the last lifeboat. The father, "Louis Hoffman," didn't survive. The boys arrived in New York on the *Carpathia*. But nobody knew who they were. No family was found.

In fact, "Louis Hoffman" wasn't the father's real name. It was Michel Navratil. Navratil took the boys from their mother in France and decided to start a new life with them in America. He didn't want their mother to know. Finally, the mother saw her sons in a newspaper, and the boys were sent back to France. There they told her their father's last words: "Tell her that I loved her and still do."

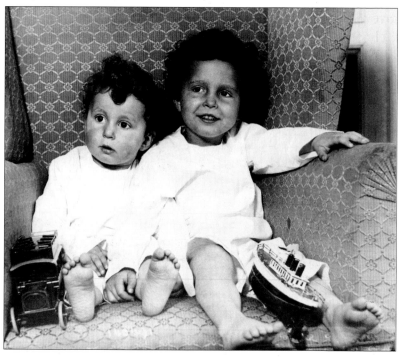

The Navratil boys.

An Unbelievable Story

Alice Cleaver was a nurse, traveling on the *Titanic* with a family in first class. The Allisons didn't know that, years earlier, Alice killed her own child. But now, she was helping to look after the Allisons' two children, Trevor and Loraine.

On the night of the accident, the Allisons went on deck. Alice Cleaver acted quickly. She picked up the baby, Trevor. "I won't let him out of my arms," she told the boy's mother. Then she left and found a lifeboat.

After she got on the *Carpathia*, she kept Trevor Allison with her. All the newspapers called her very brave. But the Allison family thought that Trevor's parents died on the ship because they were looking for their son. Their other baby, Loraine, died with them. Was Alice Cleaver using Trevor to save herself? It is true that people with babies got into lifeboats more easily.

Years later, the mystery about Alice Cleaver and the Allison family became even stranger. In 1940, an American woman, Loraine Kramer, spoke on the radio. Her story was hard to believe. She was Loraine Allison! This was her story:

A man on the *Titanic* carried her into a lifeboat. This man was the ship's builder, Thomas Andrews! He and Loraine lived together in America. Sometimes Bruce Ismay, the president of the White Star Line, visited them. He wanted them to hide because they knew important secrets about the *Titanic*.

Kramer was probably not Loraine Allison. She was probably looking for money. In fact, many people think that Alice Cleaver helped her with information about the real Loraine Allison.

Interest in Loraine Kramer's story showed that, years after the accident, people were still interested in the *Titanic*. The world saw one world war and then another, and the great ship lay in darkness at the bottom of the Atlantic. But many people dreamed of finding the *Titanic* again.

"Leave it there."

The ocean was 4,000 meters (13,120 feet) deep where the *Titanic* lay. The water was black. Some people tried to find the ship, but without success.

In 1985, Robert Ballard and Jean Jarry were looking for the ship. There were twenty-three crew and twenty-three scientists on their ship, the *Knorr*. The team was using a submarine without a crew to search the bottom of the ocean. They worked for weeks and found nothing.

Then, on September 1, they saw pieces of metal on the ocean floor. Soon they couldn't believe what the camera was showing them. There was a big, dark shape in the water. It was the front part of the *Titanic*! The crew and scientists of the *Knorr* were silent for a minute, as they remembered the dead of the *Titanic*.

When the ship was discovered, some of the mysteries of the *Titanic* were solved:

- The front part of the ship lay 600 meters (1,970 feet) from the back. So the *Titanic* did break in two as it sank. Before the ship was discovered, people weren't sure about this.
- The ship sank 21 kilometers (13 miles) from the position that Jack Phillips and Harold Bride gave on the radio.

Ballard and his team returned the next year to look at more of the ship. All of the wood was gone, but some things on the ship looked almost new. Ballard's pictures of the *Titanic* became very famous. But Ballard didn't bring anything up from the *Titanic*. He wanted to leave it all at the bottom of the ocean.

In 1987, the ship was visited by a team with a different idea. This time the scientists went down in the submarine. They brought 1,800 things up from the *Titanic*. A box from the ship was even opened on a French TV show. It was empty.

Many of the survivors were angry about all of this. When Ballard was asked for his opinion, he said, "In a word, sad." This didn't stop the French team returning a few years later. They brought 3,600 things up from the *Titanic*.

What will the future of the *Titanic* be? One business man wants to sell trips to the ship. Will anyone ever bring the ship back up from the bottom of the ocean? Survivor Eva Hart hoped not. Before her death in 1996, she said, "Leave it there."

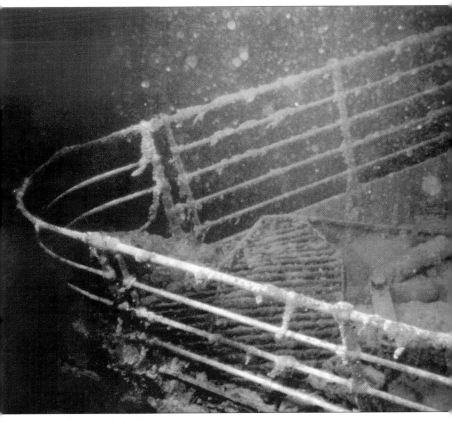

Ballard's view of the Titanic.

The *Titanic* on Film

When James Cameron was writing the movie *Titanic*, he wanted to show the rich history of the ship and its many true stories. He soon became sure of one thing. The love story between Rose and Jack was the most important part of the movie. If people worry about the two young lovers, they will understand the disaster more.

The movie's story doesn't begin in 1912. It starts in the present day, when Rose DeWitt Bukater is old. She thinks back to the past. The camera shows us the young Rose, when she sees the *Titanic* for the first time.

Rose DeWitt Bukater is getting on the *Titanic* in Southampton. "It doesn't look any bigger than the *Mauritania*," she says, speaking about another famous ship.

- British actress Kate Winslet played the young Rose, unhappy at the thought of her future with rich Cal Hockley (Billy Zane).
- All of the clothes here are exactly like the clothes of 1912.

Jack Dawson is a poor, young artist, traveling third class back to America from Europe.

First-class passengers listen while Jack Dawson explains his ideas about life. "Life's a gift," he says.

♦ James Cameron later said about Leonardo DiCaprio, "I didn't want Leo at first." But after Leonardo read some lines, Cameron changed his mind. "I knew he was the guy."

Soon Rose and Jack fall in love. When Rose asks Jack to draw a picture of her, she is wearing nothing except "the Heart of the Ocean" around her neck.

* This part of the movie was made on Leonardo DiCaprio's first day of filming. Important parts of a movie are often filmed at the beginning. The two actors later became good friends.

The lookouts watch as Rose and Jack are together on the deck. When they look up, they will see the terrible shape of the iceberg in front of the ship.

* Of course, this love story is a real difference between the movie and the real history of the *Titanic*. But, James Cameron explains, Rose's love for Jack plays a part in the terrible accident that follows.

As the water comes higher and higher, Jack and Rose try to escape from Cal.

- The actors in *Titanic* were often tired, wet, and cold. Later, DiCaprio described it as his hardest job.

The crew send rockets high into the dark sky—but the *Titanic* is sinking.

- In the 1958 movie *A Night to Remember*, the ship didn't break in two. Because of Ballard's work in 1985, Cameron and his team knew more about the ship's last seconds.

Jack Dawson, Rose DeWitt Bukater, and Cal Hockley weren't real people, but many of the people in the movie did exist.

The movie shows:
- Captain Smith and most of the ship's officers
- first-class passengers Molly Brown and Benjamin Guggenheim
- Bruce Ismay, the president of the White Star Line, and Thomas Andrews, the builder of the ship
- Jack Phillips and Harold Bride in the radio room

In the movie, Jack Dawson says that the cold water feels like "knives." These words come from one of the real survivors. Cameron read what many of the survivors wrote about *Titanic*. He used some of their words when he wrote the movie. It was important to James Cameron to show these real people. He carefully planned the story so everything happened in the movie at exactly the right time. Try watching Cameron's movie again after reading this book. Can you see all of the things that are true?

But there are some mistakes in every movie. While Jack and Rose are walking on the deck, you can see a small hill with a building on it behind Jack. But they are in the middle of the Atlantic Ocean!

As Rose finishes her story to Brock Lovett and his crew, the last line of her story is, "He exists now only in my memory." Later, she throws the Heart of the Ocean into the Atlantic.

At the very end of the movie, we see Rose back on the *Titanic*. She is young again, and Jack Dawson is waiting for her. The two are together again. James Cameron says that people always ask him about this. Is Rose dreaming or is she dead? Cameron's answer? "You decide."

"The world woke up . . ."

After Cameron's movie, more and more people became interested in the story of the *Titanic*. Every year there are more and more books and videos on the subject.

But why? After so many years, why are people still interested in the *Titanic*? There have been worse accidents on the ocean in the years since then. What is so special about the *Titanic*?

◆

Some people think that the sinking of the *Titanic* showed the end of one part of history and the start of another. Before the *Titanic* sank, it was a time of great hope. People felt good about the world's future. Buildings were becoming taller, machines were becoming faster, and, of course, ships were becoming bigger and bigger. Anything seemed possible.

◆

For many people, that dream of a wonderful future sank with the *Titanic*. After April 15, 1912, the world seemed a different place. Just two years later, the First World War began. Millions of people died. New machines were used to kill more and more people.

◆

Maybe *Titanic* survivor Jack Thayer was right when he wrote, "The world woke up on April 15, 1912."

ACTIVITIES

Pages 1–11

Before you read

1 Find these words in your dictionary. They are all in this book.

captain   crew   float   iceberg   officer   servant sink   submarine

Which words describe:

a jobs on a ship?

b what things do in water?

c things that are in or under the water?

2 What do you think the words in *italics* mean? Check in your dictionary.

a A *model* of the ship is used in the movie.

b Take this *rope* and tie the boat to that tree.

c I *survived* a fire and a car crash last year.

3 How much do you know about the *Titanic*? Try to answer the questions on page 1.

After you read

4 Discuss why the *Titanic* was called the "Ship of Dreams."

Pages 12–29

Before you read

5   What do you want to know about the accident on
   April 14, 1912? Write five questions. As you read, look
   for the answers to your questions.

6   Find these words in your dictionary. Put them in the
   sentences below.

   ahead   disaster   gentleman   operator
   upside-down   warning

   Which words go in these sentences?

   a   The heavy rain was a . . . . . for poor farmers.
   b   Go straight . . . . . and then turn left.
   c   The boat floated . . . . . in the water.
   d   A . . . . . is always polite.
   e   There is a health . . . . . on packs of cigarettes.
   f   Radio . . . . . listen for messages from other ships.

7   Find these words in your dictionary.

   lifebelt   lookout   rocket

   Which word describes:

   a   a job on a ship?
   b   something that helps people swim?
   c   something that you can see in the sky?

After you read

8   What do you think about the rule "Women and children
   first!"? Explain your thoughts.

9   Most of the lifeboats didn't go back to help people in
   the water. Why not? What were the reasons for and
   against returning?

Before you read

10 In your opinion, why did the accident happen? Pick the reason that you think is most important.

11 Tell a friend the story of Jack and Rose in James Cameron's movie *Titanic*.

After you read

12 Many things were brought up from the *Titanic* and shown to people. How do you feel about this?

13 Why did James Cameron show a love story in the movie *Titanic*? Do you agree with his reasons?

Writing

14 Imagine that you are Jack Thayer. Write a letter to Milton Long's parents. Tell them about their son and about the night of the disaster.

15 There is a new plan to bring the *Titanic* up from the bottom of the ocean. Write a letter to a newspaper, giving your feelings about the plan.

16 Write a new part of the movie. Choose something that really happened on the *Titanic* or the *Carpathia*.

17 Imagine that you work for a video magazine. Write about James Cameron's *Titanic*. Think about what you know of the real disaster. Give your opinion of the movie.

Answers to questions on page 1:

1 a   2 b   3 b   4 c   5 b   6 b   7 a   8 a   9 b   10 c